Frameless Windows,
Squares of Light

BY CATHY SONG

PICTURE BRIDE

Frameless Windows, Squares of Light

P O E M S

Cathy Song

W.W. NORTON & COMPANY

NEW YORK   LONDON

Grateful acknowledgment is made to the following publications in which some of these poems first appeared:

Amerasia Journal: "Living Near the Water."
American Poetry Review: "A Child's Painting."
Black Warrior Review: "A Small Light."
Breaking Silence: "The Day You are Born," "Losing Track."
Chaminade Literary Review: "Shadow Figures."
Columbia: "A Mehinaku Girl in Seclusion," "What Belongs to You."
Homegrown: "The Wind in the Trees."
Poetry: "The Age of Reptiles," "Litany," "The Tree House," "The Window and the Field."
Seneca Review: "Frameless Windows, Squares of Light," "Waterwings."

My love and thanks to John Unterecker whose kind and intelligent spirit has guided so many.

Published simultaneously in Canada by Penguin Books Canada Ltd., 2801 John Street, Markham, Ontario L3R 1B4.
Printed in the United States of America.

The text of this book is composed in 10.5/12.5 CRT Century Old Style, with display type set in Century Old Style.
Composition and manufacturing by The Haddon Craftsmen, Inc.
Book design by Margaret M. Wagner

First Edition

LIBRARY OF CONGRESS CATALOGING IN PUBLICATION DATA
Song, Cathy, 1955–
    Frameless windows, squares of light.
    I. Title.
PS3569.06539F7   1988   811'.54   87–28243

ISBN 0-393-02567-5

W. W. Norton & Company, Inc., 500 Fifth Avenue, New York, N. Y. 10110
W. W. Norton & Company Ltd., 37 Great Russell Street, London WC1B 3NU

1 2 3 4 5 6 7 8 9 0

for J.A. and R.E.

Contents

The Window
and the Field

THE DAY YOU ARE BORN

There was an emptiness
   waiting for you. The night
      your mother knew you existed,
she felt a flicker of sadness
   for the life, no bigger than her thumbnail,
      burrowing itself within her body.
She knew you would be
   her last child, the last flowering
      before the pod, like a crippled hand,
withered shut; the body becoming silent,
   the eggs mature and ripe,
      pungent and salty as caviar.

The night she knew
   of your existence, the small town
      slept in the blue black darkness
of eucalyptus trees and orchids.
   There was no moon to light
      the road your father would take,
spiraling in slow circles toward home.
   The key to his tailor shop
      hung from his neck like a cross.
He wore it constantly
   and the expression that went with it,
      the mournful mask of an immigrant.

If, upon returning,
   he went to the room where she slept,
      instead of walking past her door
carrying his shoes like a thief,
   he might have witnessed
      something of the grief she felt

for you who would be
    his third son, his fifth child.
        The boy who would dream
of a landing place as he crossed the river
    at night, his left hand
        assured by the worn railing of the bridge.
He would come to know its varied surface
    as it led him to the field
        where bombers maneuvered
in the searchlit sky. There in that field
    you dreamed of destinations,
        names received from the wireless,
as the planes disappeared,
    leaving the sound of their engines
        and a boy turning slowly home.

They were to call you
    their thin soldier of the homefront
        where you were to remain
interpreting the war news for your father
    who would be by then already old.
        You would always think of him as old,
sitting in his chair,
    swatting the flies with a newspaper
        while you pinpointed on the map
the names of islands
    as complicated as the legs
        of an insect. Islands where
your two brothers crept
    in a blue black darkness
        that reminded them of home.

4

Each morning you would stand
    before the injustice of love
        as your mother dressed her thin soldier
in a white starched shirt.
    Each night she steam pressed
        the white clean collar.
The iron's hiss, an asthmatic's compress,
    seemed to sear a hole in your heart,
        and the punishment it brought
when like a sickly angel you descended
    upon the chicken dirt of the school yard.
        Impressed by the mother whose child
returned each morning to stand at the gate immaculate,
    the teacher kept you at your desk
        during the noon recess. The maps you drew
flowered freely in your hand. You delayed your departure
    until the huddle of children scattered,
        comfortable in their anonymous rags.

Your father would die uneventfully
    but your mother, perched on the porch
        with a piece of sewing on her lap,
would be there waiting
    for a boy to walk home
        in the late afternoon light,
dragging his leather satchel
    behind him as if it were an anchor
        from which his shadow would rise
magnified and serene.
    The wind blows with the sound of eggshells
        the day you are born.

THE BINDING

We love them more than life,
these children who are born to us.

How did Mary endure it?
It was more than she bargained for,
the white lily light,
the passive acceptance of the sacred seed.
For the daughter of the well at dusk,
it was a moment of vanity.
He had taken notice.

He was like the stranger
who rides into town,
who in his worldliness
sees the gullible girl
and sweeps her off her feet.
He takes her by storm,
there is nothing subtle about him,
the whirlwind courtship,
the messengers trumpeting exotic flowers.

The night she opened the window,
it was raining flowers,
as she knew it would be,
and it covered her,
like a wedding dress,
like snow.

But the child in her arms was real.
The weight of him was real.
And in her diligence—
the setting of the evening bread upon the table,

the terror any mother feels
in a crowded marketplace
when for an instant
she thinks her child is missing—
she thought
He might relent, choose another,
and she could live anonymously with her son
among the dwellers of the earth,
the carpenters, the fishermen, and the thieves.

Once she held him, she was lost.
Her body turned against her,
was made maternal
so that she saw nothing else
but the child who walked further each day into light.
How could she have known this?
That the son would resist her
every attempt to bind him,
that in his loneliness he would belong
to everyone and to no one,
forfeit what welled within her
in order to save the nameless, the cripple, the unspeakable.

She was duped into thinking
when the time came
she could give the child up,
and in exchange for the son, her sacrifice,
she could receive the heavenly reward:
immortality,
candles and cathedrals,
inexhaustible light—
the thousand statutes of herself.

Who could want such eternal life?
Better the grunt and toil,
the hog's blissful sleep,
a child who needed her.
She prayed that He might forget the pact.
And then the praying stopped.
Why call attention to herself?
Let silence be her accomplice
and with the less devout she could slip
unnoticed with her son toward a simpler destiny.
Like fugitives, always under the cover of night.

In the son's greatest hour,
he loved her
not more, not less
than he loved the soldier who wept at his feet.
It was cruel to ask that of her,
of any woman allowed to bear that weight.

LITANY

She gave you the names of things,
each word, a candle
you held between yourself and the dark.
The litany of the alphabet
like a rosary before sleep.
Then the shadows on the wall
became familiar,
the storybook shape of elephants.

Mornings she took in laundry,
arms buried in suds,
her sleeves rolled up like a man.
She had no use for singing.
What she did, she did
because of you,
her last wish granted:
the midnight birth,
a boy without a breath that wasn't her own.

You were the center of her brisk movements,
the point between the porch and the tree,
the smallest insistence of color.
Your small frame, remote
as a sundial, was obedient
noon without shadow.
In a starched white shirt of silence,
you longed for a river:
a boy with a stick and a dog.

Beside the green water of the ditch,
the tall grass hid the white waxy flower.
The nights were cool and filled with its smell,

the nights you leaned out as if to test the wind,
scattering breadcrumbs,
a promise of wheat.
But the wind was never right.

What was it like
to lie down in the ditch,
your head on that hard pillow,
to hear the sound of the work
she made for herself,
the stubborn light of her window,
a burning hole she stitched in the night?

You were the one she called Andrew,
handsome and true,
the boy she called home to supper,
wiping his shoes
before a feast of fruit and flowers.
The one in the photograph
standing next to her,
winged-collar of an angel,
his hand on her sleeve,
tethered there
beside the straight-backed chair.

Guilt is a halo of silence,
the white clean shirt you wore.

You are the boy standing next to her,
the one who would never leave.

THE WINDOW AND THE FIELD

There wasn't much on the island to speak of,
a red dirt road through canefields going nowhere.
Your father's life waiting for you.
In the evenings after work,
he polished his shoes.
She wasn't the girl in the polka-dot dress
you took for a spin.
What wasn't red dirt and canefields
was off-limits: her thin shoulders,
the lights from the pink hotel
distant as the surrounding reef
silently lit with shells.

Thirty years is a long time going back
for me, unborn, a quiet witness
to the pressed kiss she saved in a basement room.
Driving home,
you stalled under the stars.
The sea meant nothing to you.
It was instead the sky, an uncut road
through a field of blue.

Your father asked gently
how the time was spent.
You offered clean hands,
a pantomime of wings above the tablecloth.
The recital of nights
you taught yourself to fly
in an abandoned field.
He lifted his eyes
and then lowered them in grace.
He remained that way unconvinced

by the girl who would come to call him father,
by your maiden flight across the dreary plates.

You speak in lengths of decades,
polishing your shoes,
as if only yesterday you carried
a young bride up the steps of the family porch.
She remembers it differently.
Red dirt and clouds
and a red dog limping toward her.
She waved but you were already down the road,
spinning a reckless veil of dust.
It was four o'clock in the trees.
A river of heat shimmered through the canestalks.

I am a part of that mixed blessing:
a pinch of salt
thrown over a weary shoulder.
If you had looked in the rearview mirror,
you might have seen it: the white gloved hand
like a white flag waving.
The day she turned slowly toward the house,
you returned in a borrowed plane,
swooping low three times in a rush of air.
The laundry fluttered.
The chickens squawked for shelter.
She carried a black suitcase up the stairs,
unlatching the door with the word father,
a man who sat far back in his chair.
She unpinned her hat, peeled off her gloves,
splitting apart the white petals.
They lay on her lap like gardenias,

twin flowers,
one for each daughter she would give you.
One patient, the other pliant:
beside the window and the field,
a self already divided.

LIVING NEAR THE WATER

He lived near the water
most of his life
which gave him the smell of the sea.
His body had grown furry
with a soft blue gray covering of hair.
His bare feet seemed rooted to the grass
where the toenails had thickened
into the ebony shell of snails.
In his lawn chair, he appeared
mammoth and prehistoric.

The day before he died,
we were sitting beside him in the yard.
The day was clear and ending and
we could feel the presence of water
as if waves were boiling right off shore.
There was the odor of salt burning,
of some drowsy spice between the trees.
The radio was on,
the dial set fuzzily between two channels.
He had been listening to the static
as though he were waiting to decipher
a message he would know
at the moment of his hearing it.
The tiny hairs in his ears, insectlike,
registering an imperceptible music.
In his right hand he held a flyswatter
which he waved like a wand
in between his moments of rest.
Those moments were lengthening
like the equatorial light of summer.

The children squirmed. The mosquitoes
had gone to rest beneath the leaves.

Still and distant,
he contained great mystery.
His clotted eye had seen
a world transformed by fire—
the stooped soldiers offering
a young boy strips of shredded meat
alongside the burning trees;
the night his son gently shook him
from sleep to witness
the astronauts somersaulting on the moon.
And in the pinpoint blue of his iris,
like snow falling inside a paperweight,
was the day his young man's eyes had scanned
the cargo of brides
who bowed before the grim life held out to them;
sucking in their breath
at the vision of their own faces
caught like orange blossoms
in the sad hands of laborers.
Those of us assembled on that day
had descended from that moment of regret;
my grandmother stepping forward
to acknowledge her own face
was the last to give herself away.

He was tired.
He had traveled in silence
since the day her eyes had fallen

upon his ill-fitting suit, his borrowed shoes.
From that moment she gave everything away.
He had traveled so long in silence
that when he turned and said,
"I love you" to my father
who was holding the youngest red-faced child,
he had clicked off the radio,
he was saying goodbye.
And then he grew thirsty,
having carried that stone on his tongue
that he moved to reach for his water.
I watched my father
bring the cup to his father's mouth, watched
how it was the son's hand that trembled.
The children were put to sleep
and while we dreamed, my father
was still holding the hand long after
the warm wind had passed through him;
flowing out through each of us,
the smell of the sea.

A Small Light

MAGIC ISLAND

A collar of water
surrounds the park
peninsula at noon.
Voices are lost in
waves of wind
that catch a kite and keep
it there in the air
above the trees.
If the day has one color,
it is this:
the blue immersion of horizons,
the sea taking the sky like a swimmer.

The picnickers have come
to rest their bicycles
in the sprawling shade.
Under each tree,
a study in small pleasures:
a boy,
half in sunlight,
naps with his dog;
a woman,
marking a page with a leaf,
squints up
to bite into an apple.

It is a day an immigrant
and his family might remember,
the husband taking off his shirt
to sit like an Indian
before the hot grill.
He would not in his own language

call it work, to cook
the sticks of marinated meat
for his son circling a yarn
of joy around the chosen tree.
A bit of luck has made him generous.
At this moment in his life,
with the sun sifting through
the leaves in panes of light,
he can easily say he loves his wife.
She lifts an infant
onto her left shoulder as if
the child is a treasured sack of rice.
He cannot see her happiness,
hidden in a thicket of blanket
and shining hair.
On the grass beside their straw mat,
a black umbrella,
blooming like an ancient flower,
betrays their recent arrival.
Suspicious of so much sunshine,
they keep expecting rain.

STAMP COLLECTING

The poorest countries
have the prettiest stamps
as if impracticality were a major export
shipped with the bananas, t-shirts, and coconuts.
Take Tonga, where the tourists,
expecting a dramatic waterfall replete with birdcalls,
are taken to see the island's peculiar mystery:
hanging bats with collapsible wings
like black umbrellas swing upside down from fruit trees.
The Tongan stamp is a fruit.
The banana stamp is scalloped like a butter-varnished seashell.
The pineapple resembles a volcano, a spout of green on top,
and the papaya, a tarnished goat skull.

They look impressive,
these stamps of countries without a thing to sell
except for what is scraped, uprooted and hulled
from their mule-scratched hills.
They believe in postcards,
in portraits of progress: the new dam;
a team of young native doctors
wearing stethoscopes like exotic ornaments;
the recently constructed "Facultad de Medicina,"
a building as lack-lustre as an American motel.

The stamps of others are predictable.
Lucky is the country that possesses indigenous beauty.
Say a tiger or a queen.
The Japanese can display to the world
their blossoms: a spray of pink on green.
Like pollen, they drift, airborne.
But pity the country that is bleak and stark.

Beauty and whimsey are discouraged as indiscreet.
Unbreakable as their climate, a monument of ice,
they issue serious statements, commemorating
factories, tramways and aeroplanes;
athletes marbled into statues.
They turn their noses upon the world, these countries,
and offer this: an unrelenting procession
of a grim, historic profile.

THE FOURTH OF JULY

Because every window is open, made public,
a bird could veer from the flock,
dive down, fly through the house and
still catch up by the time
his more timid cousins would begin
to miss his presence.
(The stunningly brave are unusually quiet.)
The listless three of us
would welcome the cooling results
of such a momentary breeze through the house.
And if the bird's irregular route were discussed,
there'd be agreement:
things turn reckless with a rising thermostat.

We eliminate the nighttime prowlers from our thoughts
(burglars and furry insects alike),
leaving the doors open, unlocked
(a sailboat waiting out the doldrums
with every sail slack but intact),
poised to snare a little wind.
It is a half-hearted attempt.
We stand before the icebox
in bare skin that clings to our bones like saran wrap
torn between a slab of baloney or another beer,
while our mountain cousins prop their poles
against a convenient rock
(poised to catch a little fish),
bend over brand-new coolers
to make the weekend's ultimate decision:
sugar-free or lite?

At midnight, still no sign of wind,
the occupants bail out
(the house barely afloat
after the day's thoughtless ins and outs;
the screen door having spanked
the back of the house at least three dozen times).
Pillows fly out of windows.
Pitched into the dark
they land on the lawn like lifeboats.
The grass is as cool as water.
A twisted sheet aids one
then another refugee.
A wave of laughter
splashes up, revives them
as a father and his three-year-old
dive into a back yard tent
(anchored safely in a bay of roses).
The moon is kind.
It stays on until dawn like a neighbor's porch light.

A CHILD'S PAINTING

What crossed his mind
when he added this?
A glimpse of sky of blue
so pale
it seems diluted with vinegar,
the blue wash of an Easter egg.

Where blue runs into black,
a collision occurs,
a feathery explosion,
the inky spray of a jellyfish.

It all seems so casual
as if his mind were on something else,
the prospect of soup and crackers,
a walk to feed the pigeons in the park.
Perhaps he was only killing time
the way another
child might de-wing a fly
or hold a shard of glass
to feel the sun's needle in the eye.

In one corner,
what was done without a brush,
a gray smear,
a midnight comet,
a breathless fingerprint
trails off the paper
onto an imaginary table
as if the child had wanted
to leave some crumbs:
This is where I went.

And changed his mind.
For look at this circle of pink.
It blooms in the center like a mouth
calling back the colors—
Did something frighten him?—
all the colors of a private alphabet.

SYMPHONY

Two days after Christmas
a light snow fell.
It fell like notes from the sky,
chaotic and random to the untrained eye.
The clock on the kitchen wall kept time.

The woman who watched it, interpreted it.
She likened it to something symphonic,
the musical texture of the snow—
a flurry of feathers in the downward descent,
the unexpected updraft, fluty, almost fragrant,
and then the insertion of the glacial pause,
the oboe's lugubrious chill.
She had been writing in her diary
when the concert began;
when she looked up,
the pen stayed still in her hand.

Nothing disturbed the drizzle of snow.
The houses lay mute
under a gauze-grain film of cheesecloth,
some kind of rough-spun linen.
Smoke from the chimneys
was hardly a protest,
lily-breath of children unseen

applauding the small winter acrobats'
obliviousness to the muffled monotony
as they schussed down the rooftops,
a feat of cookiecutter feet
leaving stenciled tracks as delicate as doilies,
unlike fossils, perishable and fleet.

Further defying the pull of snow,
they tiptoed along the horizontal wires
(taut as musical bars),
tiny tightrope walkers in cinnamon fur coats.
Someone acknowledged their performance,
welcomed the counterpoint,
left yesterday's toast by the fencepost.

Incongruous to the blurry drifts
and the small vanishing footprints
is the spinach fern
looking primitive and swampish
against the curtain of snow
(no longer linen but woolly now).
Into this ice age, this cavernous white,
a garbage truck strays into the backdrop.
(A herd of others has spread throughout the city.)
It heaves The Christmas Carcass—
the balding trees, the ribbon and tissue confections—
into its mechanical, fork-pronged jaw.
And with a mammoth roar,
it bears a tunnel through the snow and disappears.

LOSING TRACK

Last night I saw a documentary
on China. The camera crew
had traveled to the far western
province of Xinjiang. In the brief
green meadows of summer in the hills
I thought I recognized you,
but she was younger,
a girl who could have been your sister.
She was leaping in a game,
trying to catch the tail's end, a small boy,
in a snake of children
weaving through the tall grass.
Her long braids were flying like the tassels
tying her cotton quilted vest.
The camera almost touched her face: sturdy and earnest,
she seemed to smile against her will.

If you remained in China,
you would be pedaling an ancient
bicycle in Beijing. I received two letters.
The students were so polite
they made you feel venerable
beyond your years, waiting after class
to hand you rice cakes and panfried doughnuts.
I can hear them reciting
your stilted English sentences: at school,
I had once mistaken you for a foreigner,
your speech halting and deliberate.
You described your room, writing
how cold it was to face
the northern slant of the sun.
The light made you think of Michigan,

driving home through the woods with your father.
You made tentative plans to return
to the family house,
to finish a book of stories
you began writing in an upstairs room.
And then you wrote that you had fallen
in love with one of your students
but as if thinking it over,
you were riding an inland train
with someone else, a safe companion,
a woman with unfeminine features.

That is where we lost track
of one another. The silence that followed
your last letter grew longer,
becoming a tunnel of snow
the train you were riding whistled through.
Our words had been what had kept
us alive to one another and when they stopped,
a jade fish, an old coin,
was dropped into the blue China Sea.
Last night I found myself alone
when your face was brought back to life.
I dreamt I went to find you
in the drafty halls of the school
where in the mausoleum silence
of the library we would study, side by side,
our identical hair covering
the English language we both loved.

The story you began writing in Michigan
was a notebook you carried

across the snow quiet fields of the campus.
Walking in the shadow of the lights
along College Road, our tracks
had already begun to diverge
with our good night and a stack of books
at the frozen lily pond.
I watched you trudge up the hill
toward the observatory.
I see you as you were then,
so serious you did not mean to scowl,
your black ponytail, an ink brush,
dipping into the night air,
dotting the points to a constellation
you had yet to name.

A MEHINAKU GIRL IN SECLUSION

When the pequi fruit blossomed,
I went into seclusion.
A red flower
dropped out of my body
and stained the red dirt of the earth
one color. With one color
I became married to the earth.
I went to live by myself
in the hut at the end of the village.

There no one must see me.
For three years,
no one must touch me.
The men carve the spirit birds
and dream of me
becoming beautiful in the dark.
They say my skin
will be as delicate as the light
that touches the spider's web.
The women walk to the river
and bathe and time passes.

One woman, the old one,
brings me news of the harvest,
the names of the children who are born.
The children are taught
to make babies out of mud,
babies in the shape of gourds.
The children cry when the rains come.

When the rain comes I slip out
and circle the dirt plaza.

I pause as if to drink at each door.
At each door,
the sound of the sleeping.
I return before the first
hint of light,
return to hear
the click of my spinning.

I will learn to become
mistress of the hammocks.
The man who will be my husband
shall be proud.
When I walk beside him
to bathe in the river,
I will say with my body,
He is mine.
The manioc bread he eats
becomes the children I will bear.
His hammocks are not tattered.
Ask him. Yes, ask him.
I am learning to say this
with my body.

A SMALL LIGHT

When the man comes home he takes off his hat
and looks up at the leaves of the tree.
The light annoints each leaf as it sinks into the sea.
The tree shimmers like a thousand mirrors,
the suddenness of birds in flight.
A child is sleeping in the house.
The house rises and falls with each breath
as if the house were made of cloth.
Tacked to the walls is the sound of the clock
which keeps the house from floating away.
A curtain divides the bed and the sink.
A woman lies on the bed and feels
the house fall into itself, the window fill with leaves.
Her body fills with sleep
as if sleep were a dream of water.
The sound of the clock grows smaller
like a light in a window you pass at night.
The child opens her eyes to a dream of water.
A web in the window is sunlight
seen from the inside of water.
Floating in the window, it is barely there,
like her breath, like hair.
She understands what can't be seen
can still be broken.
She holds her breath as though her breath
could break. When the tree hauls its leaves
in shadows across the room,
the web stretches like an accordian,
but silent, elastic, made of skin.
A dead stream is a river of leaves.
All day the wind stirs a parched soup,
a kindling of matchsticks and leaves,

the size of the child's hand.
Some part of the tree is always dying.
Somewhere it is always raining leaves
and a child, closing the door on the falling
walls of a house, walks away,
her slight dress sinking into the dry river,
hair, a small light, touching each leaf.

Shadow Figures

SHADOW FIGURES

1.
For a few moments in history
we were close, like twins
whispering without lights,
telepathic:
you in the top bunk,
your slight body
wheezing in the wind
stirring pollen.
We listened for the dog's
scratching on the screen,
etching metallic messages
with a deliberate paw.
The pink calloused skin
padded to our corner of the house,
his collar bell jingling
like money in the pocket.

Fifteen years later,
another boy walks out of the house.
He is selling a litter of kittens.
I hold one,
feeling the delicate bones
curl in my hand.
My father and three Tongans
built this wall,
I will never tell this boy
with peach colored hair.
And the bougainvillea they transplanted
from a seedling has grown
extravagant with age,
spilling a waterfall of blossoms,

purple and fuchsia.
I see the matchstick house,
riddled with termites,
had a luxuriance
my brother and I imagined.
But the sense of refuge was real.

2.
In similar weather,
mist pressing close to earth,
there is a stillness
to the afternoon I remember
in Golden Gate Park
when we were very young.
My brother was feeding rice
crackers to the squirrels
nibbling their way to his hand
laid on the grass,
still and unafraid.
He was small and smooth,
calm as a stone in a garden,
full and oval in its contemplation
as if all of its life
it had absorbed the sound of rain.
We called my brother Mahatma Gandhi
because he was thin and dark.
We called him Gandhi
for the eggplant hue of his slight body
against the pale soles of his feet.

This was before
we moved into adolescence

and into separate rooms.
When you were no longer here
but buried beneath
a quilt of comics,
wearing headsets that made
you look like an insect.
On Saturdays I knew
where to find you—
knees bent, stroking
the chalky fur of the terrier
whose tongue flicked
like a pink ribbon.
He seemed content to wait
at your side, forever
if you had wished,
for the soggy tennis ball
to be thrown one last time
across the yard.

3.
"Look how he loves us!"
we said
as the dog humped our legs.
He had the yard,
the pool (his water dish),
the cool dirt beneath the trees.
Then days when he saw no one
but our mother hanging the morning wash.

High-strung,
heartflutter of a hummingbird,
he longed for the great escape.

He jumped out of our arms
and missed the gate;
misjudged the shrub's height.
A slipped disk and
a chicken wire barricade
reinforced his persistence.
He was bold about his intentions:
dug a mine field of trenches
in the back yard.
He was forty-nine in dog years,
an old man,
by the time he finally made it,
tunneling across to the other side.
After a week,
he returned scruffy and beat.

4.
He died a year later.
One day after school
we turned the corner to find
the gate unlatched,
swinging open like a gaping jaw.
We flung our books
and ran into the silent yard,
the spool of dread unwinding
as though we were held
pinned under water.
The blood hammered in my throat.
The shelter of years we built
had sapped his instinct.
When the neighbor's sheep dog
clamped its teeth,

it was a bear trap
locking rust and death
around the hind leg of a rabbit.

I heard your voice that night
like a high pitched frequency
call his name,
your body poised like an antenna
on top of the jungle gym.
Twelve years old,
your body a flag of grief.

We lived in that house
for many years.
But after the death,
I never knew
what came to replace for you
that small intelligent animal.
His quick ears picking out
the pulse of your sleep.
In this life,
this is what we have—
the two of us
in the interval we call childhood—
shadow figures in a matchstick house.

HUMBLE JAR

My mother kept them in a jar
at the bottom of her sewing chest
beneath the trays of thread,
the ragged toothed scissors,
the ditto marker (a tiny replica of a pizza cutter),
and the pale pink pincushion
trimmed with Chinese acrobats
enduring a hail of needles across their laps.

There at the bottom
in a mayonnaise jar
were the buttons,
smooth and cool as the mints
she hid in the glove compartment of the car.

She had a button for every emergency,
the way she just happened to have
a band-aid in her wallet
or some chewing gum in a back pocket.
She'd bring these out as if by magic,
waving a tootsie roll like a wand.
To a tired and grumpy child
in the middle of an asphalt parking lot
such tricks of foresight
went unapplauded.
On an airplane,
among many feats of first aid
was mending a torn hem:
out came a sewing kit as portable as a matchbook.
She could easily have led
the double life of a spy.

Useful yet undervalued
was the common currency of white,
the button that could always do in a pinch—
on my school blouses,
on my father's short sleeve shirts.
They were plain and modest,
unremarkable but reliable,
rescuing a garment at a moment's notice.
They filled the jar like pennies.

Others were less practical,
the buttons that had been lost
and then retrieved,
only to reenter the orphanage,
the original setting (a cashmere coat,
a bottle-green evening gown) long gone,
shipped off to Goodwill
with the other ousted heirlooms:
the denture-pink Melmac plates and cups.
What remained was no longer a button
but a relic—
a coat of arms,
a silver dollar—
something you couldn't spend.

She prized the leather ones,
braided and varnished
like the miniature strudels
my dolls secretly enjoyed with tea.
Her indestructible car coat
was on the third generation of these.

Rarer still were the metal ones,
the flat disks of gold
that had once tailored
a navy blue suit.
I held these to my ears
as if they were the earrings she never wore,
offering them to a younger self,
a child's soft face in the mirror,
gazing back, almost beautiful.

She displayed seashells on a bureau,
an absent-minded collection of many vacations
placed like a bowl of fruit
on a tea-stained doily.
But the buttons,
stashed in that jar,
were oddly private.
She'd never admit it.
She'd say they had their uses.
A dip into that humble jar
repaired a shirt,
but it also retrieved a moment
out of a cluttered life—
before I was born,
before any of us had made our claims.
The summer she wore that scalloped dress,
she turned and smiled for the camera,
my father, for life that was certain to be glorious.
Beginners, both of them, the blind leading the blind.

THE VEGETABLE AIR

You're clean shaven in this country
where trees grow beards of moss,
where even bank tellers
look a little like banditos
in vests as pungent as sweatsuits.
Still, you prefer the vegetable air
to almost any other place on the map.
After the heart attack,
you considered Paris—
the flying buttresses,
the fractured light of its cathedrals;
the entire city refined and otherworldly,
ascending on its architectural wings—
but decided you had no use for glory,
boulevards fur-lined
with statues and expensive trees.

You admit, on the whole,
the towns in this country are ugly.
One summer you drove toward Nicoya
(a beautiful name that became your destination),
expecting a fragrant town of mango trees
but found cattle grazing in the plaza,
rattling the tin plates
in the ubiquitous Chinese restaurant.
A Coca-Cola sign hung weathered and askew.
That's perhaps why you like it,
it's a country you can't count on,
a country of misfits.
Unable to take root in the mud,
the twentieth century has failed miserably,
creating neither factory nor industry

but a thirst for soda pop;
like cosmetic surgery,
it is skin deep.
The clock is stuck in the rain
and the mud of four o'clock.
There's nothing to do but wait as if
in a dry cave, a room with a view of the waterfall,
pinned as you are beneath the downpour.
The waiter bends over your cup
without filling it,
the storekeeper holds your change
until the rain, hypnotic and dramatic,
leaves the streets and the gutters,
the balcony and the air greener, heavier—
mildew blooming in the closet where your shoes,
powdered with a sea-green lichen,
resembles old bronze,
a pair of ancient goblets.

While iguanas lounge in the attic
(a prehistoric version of the domestic rat),
the Office of the Ministry
(a pink and crumbling building
surrounded by dusty rose trees)
prints more money to prop
the flimsy flowered currency.
You can't predict what your American
dollars will bring by morning.
In the hotel restaurant
you meet the Undesirable American.
He learns just enough of the local lingo

to swing by, living on a dwindling account
and, here and there, a real estate swindle.
Or the pensionado who buys two cigars,
offering you one the day
his Social Security arrives.
Like the cockroach, the displaced
have crawled through the cracks
and selected for themselves
an agreeable niche.
A place to start from scratch.
They thrive in the vegetable air.
You wonder how you'll survive,
unfit, unable to work.
Lacking the predatory skills,
you've stayed in the trees,
a dreamer, all your life,
even now wanting to believe
a change of scenery
will get you back on your feet.
A brief hiatus in the vegetable air.

Tonight, you walk along the damp streets,
an average steak, a glass of wine
swishing in your belly,
to your small room wedged between
a jukebox and a dance hall.
There are so many things you can't change—
like the dull thrashing music.
You draw the blinds, switch on the tiny cassette.
Silence. The click of the tape.
And then the familiar aria,

rising like the moon,
lifts you out of yourself,
transporting you to another country
where, for a moment, you travel light.

THE TOWER OF PISA

There was always something that needed fixing,
a car on the blink,
a jinxed washing machine,
a high-strung garbage disposer.
His life was one of continual repair.
He toyed with gadgets,
made them hum, churn, spin.
And when, miraculously, nothing needed him,
he set his tinkering soul onto larger schemes:
major home improvements.
He built courtyards and patios,
innumerable extentions,
doubling the size of the original bungalow,
planted olive trees outside my window.
The lattice-work of grapevines,
the frothy bougainvilleas
were his ideas: to cultivate an oasis
on a suburban street.
He didn't mind the physical work,
he was glad for it.
For a living, he spent his days
strapped inside a cockpit,
shuttling tourists from one island to another,
with not even a tsunami
to relieve the monotony of a routine
take-off, a routine three-point landing.
Never a cloud in that tropical sky,
nothing so much as a stray nene bird on the runway
to test his true ability.
A boy who had wanted nothing else
but to fly those gorgeous machines.
It was maddening, the inactivity,

the call to mediocrity. Any idiot,
he insisted, can sit and steer on automatic pilot.
Those were the days he chomped furiously
on big cigars and snacksize Hershey bars.

So weekends found him scrunched on the kitchen floor
amid a chaos of nuts and bolts and screws,
with no manual to guide him—
a Chinese torture puzzle to me,
sweet labor to him.
Or hammering as if his life depended on it,
his mouth bristling with nails.
I'd get dizzy watching him at that great height,
on top a rickety, paint-splattered ladder,
swaying like the Tower of Pisa.
I was always afraid he'd hurt himself,
die and leave us unprepared.
When I was six, I witnessed
a pickax slam into his right hand,
how with a sharp intake of breath—
he made no other sound—
he reversed the action, the miscalculation,
in grueling slow motion.
I knew he needed protecting.
I was convinced of it.
From that moment, I became his shadow,
a pair of eyes on the lookout
for imminent catastrophe,
scanning the yard for possible pitfalls—
removing shovels, nails, bear-clawed weeders
from his path,
anchoring the flimsy ladder as he descended,

gropingly, paint or sawdust in his eyes.
I was never far from his ferocious energy.
On my bicycle I'd patrol the patio and the pool,
anticipating any threat of danger.
He thought I had nothing better to do—
How could he interpret my devotion?—
and he'd send me on errands
which would worry me,
leave him unguarded.
He'd call me Speedy Gonzalez
when I'd bring, in record time, iced tea,
cloudy with saccharine the way he liked it.
See? I'd tell myself, nothing happened.
I went, was gone, he's still here,
alive, sprinkled with sawdust,
thirsty, a man of forty-five.
A year later he suffered a myocardial infarction.
He was flying between two islands
when, like a piece of shrapnel, the pain hit.
When he landed, he drove himself to the hospital.

What makes a child sense a parent's fragility?
What I had seen years ago had been dramatic enough:
the gashed hand brimming with blood.
But it seems gentler than that,
a kind of eavesdropping,
when I saw in my father someone else,
a man who, night after night,
after he thought we were asleep,
would play the same recording of *La Bohème,*
softly so as not to wake us,
and go out into the yard.

I listened as the music
flowed through my room
on its way toward him,
sitting on a lawn chair in the dark,
poised to receive the perfect pitch,
each aria projecting him somewhere I could not reach:
stunned at my body's resistance to make music.
The flat refusal.

It was the striving for perfection,
wasn't it,
and the falling short
that made him return each night
to the one source of beauty that consoled him,
the untiring devotion of the human soul,
distilled in the purest vibrato
that sings undiminished,
unhampered there above the trees.
And he could weep because of it,
because he thought he was alone.

He says I saved my own life
that day I fell into the pool.
I'm not so sure.
I was riding my bicycle
with one eye on him
when I toppled in.
I hadn't yet learned to swim.
I would've stayed at the bottom—
for a second, I was resigned to it—
were it not for his arm reaching out
like a branch above the water.

I have owed him this
all my life—this worry,
this constant concern.
I was his shadow,
a child trying to make sense of it all,
hinged on disaster,
a child waiting for my father to fall.

THE WIND IN THE TREES

clears the morning of doves.
You remember the loneliness,
the loneliness you knew as a child
when everyone in the house was busy.
The house would smell of frying then

and your parents would move
back and forth across the room,
their shadows overlapping like swords.
And when they were free,

remember the sunlight
on your hands,
the light and dark side of a fist.
The wind pulling on your face like water.
In a carriage you traveled anciently,

a blanket tucked around your lap.
No one asked you anything.
No one pointed out the trees.
Then as an afterthought

you were remembered and
a cracker was crumbled onto your tray.
Little Bird they called you, *Little Bird.*
You could expect a frivolous squeeze.
Perhaps a feather under the chin.

There wasn't much you wouldn't do.
Lost in the folds
of the voluminous drapes one morning

you heard someone say,
look how cleverly the child plays.

And your mother clapped pleasantly
as you scuttled back and forth,
like a beetle or a mouse,
terrified and trapped,
repeating the act.

Today you remember the loneliness
in the small figure of your son
scooting by like a clown
on a red and yellow tricycle.
His intrepid feet,
posing as pedals,

kicking up the dust of the carpet.
Say goodbye and he waves
at the children going to school.
Their lunch pails and rain jackets

are the bright objects
bobbing below the window box.
Say anything. Say love
and he will lean to press

his cheek against the floor.

ONE DAY

They come from a place far off
that you and I cannot remember.
Perhaps that is why
they seem to ask for sleep
the way a polite child
will ask for water.
The ones newly hatched.

Think of the distance
they have to travel,
landing into our laps
as if they had floated
quietly to earth like snow.
Suspended in swings from trees
when they are just days old,
they appear to us on the horizon
like parachutists in miniature,
surveying the land
they have fallen upon.

For the first three months or so,
they do not belong to us,
the other life still claims them.
They sleep and dream among the very old
who convalesce on porches,
in brittle broken rooms,
remembering moments from the life
they must soon let go.

They have no choice in the matter.
It is no small wonder

they are afraid of the dark,
fear spreading like a web
with the gradual loss of memory.
We offer them poor substitutes
like bad sweets.
This life is yet an absence
and a stream of disappearing
phantoms, sounds and shapes:
a face peering close,
a ringing bell,
wind sweeping under curtains.

One day the darkness leaves
like water receding from the town
hit by a spring storm.
Goodbye, they wave goodbye,
and turn to lead the small ones
first across the temporary bridge.
The room comes into focus.
The table, the chair,
the trees outside are at last familiar.
They move themselves to rise
from small white beds
to take the name tacked on the door.

This is the last time
they will stand so clearly
outside themselves. Years later,
if asked about the blue mark,
the one that deepens depending on the light,
they will not be able to answer.

Only: here is where the street begins,
where the houses,
opening their blue curtains
to yards crisscrossed with clothes lines,
are all that they, like you, remember.

Frameless
Windows,
Squares
of Light

THE TREE HOUSE

We knew it simply as the tree,
unremarkable, without a single flower,
without scent but the scent of itself.
Yellow was the color of the house we lived in,
one flight up the broken stairs,
the leaves began, layer upon layer
of green. Our son was the shadow,
dusk gathering under the leaves,
summer nights we breathed in the smell of it
green, the roots pulling water
in our sleep, deep within the dark green cellar.

The tree kept the house from poverty,
the limbs that held the porch in place
creaked like the screen door,
with each swing of the hammock.
We used to lie under the leaves and dream,
and what we dreamed with others
adorned the tree. The green afternoon
voice of the student soprano,
the five o'clock daughter of the piano keys,
and someone calling Jeremy home
unleashed a shower of leaves,

of coins, green and heart-shaped, into our hands.
Startled by a bird that flew one morning
into the house, we awoke to luxury,
the green years on Eustis Street,
summer and spring,
when we were in love,
still inventing our lives.
Missing the last bus from the square,

not even winter could make us feel
the poverty of the plywood chairs.
The sputtering of the gas stove
was a blue flame in the chilled branches,
smooth, shaven of leaves,
like the antlers of some gentle beast
stirring asleep beneath the snow.
The nights we walked home to the tree
and the tree was a web of stars.

WATERWINGS

The mornings are his,
blue and white
like the tablecloth at breakfast.
He's happy in the house,
a sweep of the spoon
brings the birds under his chair.
He sings and the dishes disappear.

Or holding a crayon like a candle,
he draws a circle.
It is his hundredth dragonfly.
Calling for more paper,
this one is red-winged
and like the others,
he wills it to fly, simply
by the unformed curve of his signature.

Waterwings he calls them,
the floats I strap to his arms.
I wear an apron of concern,
sweep the morning of birds.
To the water he returns,
plunging where it's cold,
moving and squealing into sunlight.
The water from here seems flecked with gold.

I watch the circles
his small body makes
fan and ripple,
disperse like an echo
into the sum of water, light and air.
His imprint on the water

has but a brief lifespan,
the flicker of a dragonfly's delicate wing.

This is sadness, I tell myself,
the morning he chooses to leave his wings behind,
because he will not remember
that he and beauty were aligned,
skimming across the water, nearly airborne,
on his first solo flight.
I'll write "how he could not
contain his delight."
At the other end,
in another time frame,
he waits for me—
having already outdistanced this body,
the one that slipped from me like a fish,
floating, free of itself.

FRAMELESS WINDOWS, SQUARES OF LIGHT

1.
Everything changed the summer your sister was born.
Your mother, suddenly slim but asymmetrical
(with your sister slung on one hip),
regained her figure and lost her sense of humor.
She snapped easily like the beans
she snipped for supper,
a succession of little flare-ups
that came and went, efficient and clean.
Her hands would pass over you in transit,
preoccupied, on their way somewhere else.
You watched them fly

the way you'd watch the birds in the evening
when a slight ruffling of the air
would lift your face toward their flight.
You'd watch them skim over rooftops,
still pools in the darkening light,
and wave after wave of trees
and feel alone in your body,
wind filling your shoes, your clothes
with the hollow sound of water.

2.
Once it had been just the two of you
cloistered in your infancy.
Days when not only winter locked you in.
The days had the solemn expectation
of a child who today opens another window,
an advent calendar's blue paper window.
Each window, a wafer of light

you could carry like a snowflake
to the darkest part of the house.

Her face, unadorned as a kitchen clock,
surveyed the white feathery weather,
measuring the distance between each hour
as carefully as she counted the cups of flour.
She'd wipe her hand across the window
so that you too could look out;
like a schoolteacher erasing a cluttered blackboard,
she'd leave a clearing,
a window framed within another,
a space for your name.

It remained, the wooden syllables,
scattered, unclaimed on the bureau
while you watched her sift the flour,
lulled into silence like a paperweight
(the cottage, the pine tree, the falling snow).
And it would be snowing on both sides of the glass,
snow sifting through her hands,
blowing across the kitchen table.

3.
You are smiling in all the pictures,
standing in the foreground
while the backdrop shifted;
like musical chairs,
places were relinquished and exchanged
until every combination was snapped.
The nurses came and went.
Flowers appeared. The baby slept on its mother's lap.

Time like a temperature was taken.
You watched the scene changes in slow motion,
the distance of figures
trudging through a falling snow.

You are smiling in the pictures
but your heart is not in it.
Your mouth forms a big O,
sweet and empty as the doughnuts
you were not allowed to eat.
You can eat anything now.
You are smiling but your heart is not in it.
You snatched it out of the picture
and gave it to the boy
who sits under the trees
(frameless windows, squares of light
float upward in the dark like luminous kites)
waiting for the words to come in.

WHAT BELONGS TO YOU

There was a river in you,
small and dark,
unseen behind the trees,
the mornings you left the house,
your mother, at last, asleep.

No one saw you walking,
as if an inch above the ground.
Your father sat at the table
and fed the rumpled dogs.
The kite pinned to your shoulder
curved lightly like your cheek
turned to the wind.
You sailed, unnoticed, into the trees.

The house had fourteen doors.
She closed each one behind her.
So she would fade by early daylight,
rejuvenated at noon.
                    There a window opened,
a map you could trace
to the sound of her sewing,
the hesitant pressure of her foot on the pedal.
Surrounded by needles and crumpled cloth,
she swayed as though she were playing the piano.

She complained of pins and needles of the body,
a head that hurt in a sky that wanted rain.
What it took to transfer the pain.
Like an acupuncturist, she poked
the little soul of the cloth,
wore a dress of penitence.

Your father hung sadly about the house,
a portrait of his father
signing checks at a faraway desk.
When he remembered, he switched on the light.

Unnoticed, you sailed into the trees
where the pull of the wind
could release your name like a kite:
calling yourself home,
flinging the broken sound of it
into the leaves
until it flew back,
indivisible,
the two syllables locked like an integer,
a black crow's constant set of wings.

This is your name,
and a river runs through it,
small and dark;
your mother singing softly to herself,
and your father, wanting very much to please,
could never decide which way,
pointing north and south,
a flimsy cross thrust in the heart of a field.
What would it take to waken them?
You watched them settle into sleep,
in unhappiness, lying side by side—
your father in his proper clothes,
your mother in a dress that would not fit—
unable to say what could save them,
a boy falling out of the trees.

TRIBAL SCENES

1.
They appear to be spear fishing,
sway-backed they stand,
ankle deep in the lime green lagoon,
naked but for poised spears
festooned with feathers.
She is about to strike,
make shishkebab of Godzilla.
Her brother yells for clemency,
he wants the creature spared.
After all, Godzilla—betrayed,
floating belly up—is still his toy.
No matter that they've been stalking him
together for the last three days.
She shrieks and jumps up and down.
I get called into the picture.
But her brother remains adamant,
the Rock of Gibraltar.
And so, Godzilla lives, barely—
flung like a beach ball onto a lawn chair—
as they've argued his fate
every day of the summer,
gesturing and grunting,
jockeying for dominance and affection,
brandishing their plastic bamboo spears.
Equipped with the primal language of siblings,
they reinvent these tribal scenes.
And when the sun hangs low in the trees,
they climb into the hammock
like spiders crawling back into a web.
Dead to the world they sleep,
limbs crossed, weapons laid down,

all trespasses forgiven.
Like twins they sleep,
side by side in alliance.

From this distance
I would say they were happy.
We belonged to each other.
The simplicity of that fact
was the call home to supper,
our names, spoken together as though they were one,
linked us forever to that flat piece of land,
the size of a handkerchief, blind-stitched
in a row of similar bungalows
one mile east of the railroad and the river.

2.
Sometimes my brother would hold me
the way my son holds onto his sister,
tightly, for practical reasons,
to keep them both from flying out of the hammock.
The look of terror on his face
is one my brother never wore
as my dare-devil daughter arches back
like a circus performer,
her hair almost touching the grass.
The loosely woven hammock
sagging beneath the leaves
was the safety net between ourselves and the earth.
It was sleek as a kayak, wobbly as a canoe.
And we would wave our arms
as though they could save us—
the ships sailing by, preoccupied, so full of purpose.

Or turn them into strokes of luck,
survivors of a shipwreck
paddling through the next typhoon.

Boredom hit
by three o'clock.
Sluggish and irritable
we limped toward the tree,
and if by luck it happened to be laundry day,
to nurse the wounds and count the loot
(bottle caps and cigarette butts),
to share the peaceful pipe—
invisible to the world in our tent,
our tepee, our magnificent hut:
the house of permanent press,
its cool damp walls of sheets and shirts
billowing around us.
Bannished together for one reason or another
(her need to be alone),
we belonged to each other,
nomads seeking temporary shelter.

3.
For something about the leaves was like the water,
the quick movement of sunlight then shadow,
the opening and closing of the tree.
We remembered it—glimpsed from the back
of a truck—the river running,
shimmering through the heat of our day;
evaporation, that mysterious process,
lending humidity, a softness to the air.
To think we could travel upon that water—

as though we could accompany each other
into life like that,
navigators cupping the light,
what little light
with our hands,
the small body of knowledge
we had gathered together—
to where? At some point
the road turned away from the river.

4.
The day you fell ill,
I watched as you were lifted into the house.
In their arms you appeared smaller,
you seemed to be floating away.
The house was turned inside out,
the living room became your domain.
For weeks you ruled from there.
A mattress was dragged onto the floor.
Pillows appeared to prop
the newly crowned king.
You lapped it up.
You never enjoyed yourself so much,
in the dramatic role of The Convalescent.
There was, after all, some future in it—
fame and fortune
(every kid on the block longed to succumb to it),
the unexpected holiday,
the endless soda pops,
Loony Tunes at three o'clock.
I could hear you laughing, laughing,
a belly of a laugh—

How could a sick kid laugh so hard?—
as if the joke was something I couldn't catch.
Secretive and suddenly privileged,
I knew you wouldn't be coming back.

Growing pains is how they would describe it,
as if you could feel your legs lengthening,
tugging at the sockets,
pulling away, inching toward the edge of the bed:
the audible sigh of the neglected houseplant
that is finally repotted.
During those weeks you grew your most at night.
When I saw you, you were taller.
I had only to be patient.
My turn would come
less successfully; in every family,
the child who resists, who grieves unnecessarily.

It was temporary,
the oasis, the shelter.
The tree was an ocean of leaves,
an inland sea,
and the world from the hammock
appeared upside down, never to right itself:
how my brother, perched on the highest branch that summer,
seemed to dive toward the sky.

HEAVEN

He thinks when we die we'll go to China.
Think of it—a Chinese heaven
where, except for his blond hair,
the part that belongs to his father,
everyone will look like him.
China, that blue flower on the map,
bluer than the sea
his hand must span like a bridge
to reach it.
An octave away.

I've never seen it.
It's as if I can't sing that far.
But look—
on the map, this black dot.
Here is where we live,
on the pancake plains
just east of the Rockies,
on the other side of the clouds.
A mile above the sea,
the air is so thin, you can starve on it.
No bamboo trees
but the alpine equivalent,
reedy aspen with light, fluttering leaves.
Did a boy in Guangzhou dream of this
as his last stop?

I've heard the trains at night
whistling past our yards,
what we've come to own,
the broken fences, the whiny dog, the rattletrap cars.
It's still the wild west,

mean and grubby,
the shootouts and fistfights in the back alley.
With my son the dreamer
and my daughter, who is too young to walk,
I've sat in this spot
and wondered why here?
Why in this short life,
this town, this creek they call a river?

He had never planned to stay,
the boy who helped to build
the railroads for a dollar a day.
He had always meant to go back.
When did he finally know
that each mile of track led him further away,
that he would die in his sleep,
dispossessed,
having seen Gold Mountain,
the icy wind tunneling through it,
these landlocked, makeshift ghost towns?

It must be in the blood,
this notion of returning.
It skipped two generations, lay fallow,
the garden an unmarked grave.
On a spring sweater day
it's as if we remember him.
I call to the children.
We can see the mountains
shimmering blue above the air.
If you look really hard

says my son the dreamer,
leaning out from the laundry's rigging,
the work shirts fluttering like sails,
you can see all the way to heaven.

THE AGE OF REPTILES

The day you are born,
your brother swings himself
high into the air.
So high, in fact,
that the rope wobbles slack
in his fall back toward earth.
To an imaginary crew he yells,
"This is the captain speaking.
Turbulence! Fasten your seat belts!"
His hair, straight and brittle,
a magnet to static electricity
and linty knots is still very yellow.
He thinks he is alone in the yard;
the world, for all he knows, is spring.

The day you are born,
your mother steps outside the house.
She is wearing a red sweater,
one that she wore all winter.
Since Valentine's, she has been watching
for signs, if this is the day
a child might take the long way home,
carrying between woolen gloves,
like a tin foiled pastry,
a homemade heart.
She herself is like a valentine,
a small red figure
waiting for a child to round the corner
and appear out of the white envelope of snow.

Some years later,
you are the stewardess

balancing a tray of teacups
as you make your way down the aisle,
the cracked sidewalk trimmed with marigolds.
Clouds glide past,
plump and complacent as cows.
You nod and smile at each dull face.
The flight is uneventful.
The pilot has gone to school.

You read his books,
listen to his radio.
Lying in your brother's room
you think you know him
by his absence, the cleft in the bed;
by the clues he left behind,
the different phases of boyhood
he devoured like comic books.
A timeline spans the length of his room.
The Age of Reptiles is the longest blue line.
Man's brief history
is less than an inch of time.
Long ago he explained it—
The Dawn of Man;
it still amazes you.
You think your own family is like that:
they appear together for a moment,
the time it takes to assemble
for a photograph,
to move toward one another.
But life is a long blue line.

The mornings he sat at the table,
his rare presence took on heroic consequences.
He ate in mythic portions:
a loaf of tuna sandwiches
stacked like a deck of cards
and a gallon of milk
would disappear under his arm
into the caverns of his room.
He'd be gone as if for days
only to reemerge, starved;
a fleet of freshly glued model airplanes—
Messerschmitts, Mustangs, and Spitfires—
drying under the lamp.
Across the hall, the rumpled
coughing of his sleep was oddly comforting.
The neutral hum of his humidifier
put the house to sleep.
You would know that sound anywhere
and the ancient smell of vapor rub
misting the rooms.

In your own time,
you entered the smooth traffic
of the household, the brief
congestion at breakfast.
The family moved in and out of the day
without collision, without
a hint of what the others dreamed.
The table was like the street at noon,
deserted but for a child

pedaling her way up the sidewalk;
her bicycle, a hand-me-down,
making a dilapidated sound.

The morning your mother stepped out
into early March, it was as if
to say goodbye to the boy in the swing
who had begun to trace his own life,
an invisible arc, away from her.
And you, where do you fit in,
born in the evening on that day in March.
You would forever want to call to them
to wait, to turn and wave
and leave open the gate.
But your brother would grow tired of the swing
and your mother, slightly chilled,
would turn to go inside.

It seems you've been looking out
one window, one moment all your life,
at the slant of roof and trees,
while everything around you evolved,
became something else.
The scissored hands of the kitchen clock
had snipped the days apart
and your brother had become
a picture on the piano.
But your lives never stopped overlapping
after all. Like the black and white movies
you both would watch together

where figures out of the past
one by one step forward to say goodbye,
he sleepwalks out of his room
and into your dream of a sad
but happy ending;
a refugee in his boyhood pajamas,
rubbing his eyes, standing at the door,
saying it's late.

Now the evenings are spent
walking the neighborhood haphazardly
in an attempt to shuffle the houses,
make them interchangeable;
so that when you come upon your own house
as if by accident, it will seem no different;
it will be with the equanimity of a stranger
looking in, seeing the room
at the top of the stairs,
a woman dozing in a spotless kitchen
where supper is being kept warm.
Before going in to take
your place at the table,
you think of all the families
you could have claimed as yours,
and you open the door
and walk into this one.